Belated Balladeer

Ballads and poems for every emotion

by
Hugh McCallion

Designed and illustrated by Sylvia Leigh

Front cover illustration from a painting of
Douglas Bridge by Mabel Foye

ISBN 0 9527920 0 1

Printed in Great Britain by H. E. Jones Ltd., Birmingham.

Published by Finnmourne Publications, 124 Hartley Road,
Kingstanding, Birmingham B44 0RE, England.

My dear old mother used to say:
  "You'll only waste your breath,
Unless you make them laugh or cry
  Or scare them half to death!"
For you, dear friend, if such it be,
This little book should do all three.

Acknowledgements

Grateful acknowledgement is made to the Editors of the
*Ulster Herald, Strabane Chronicle, Fermanagh Herald,
Donegal News, Leitrim Observer, Sunday Mercury*
and the *Birmingham Evening Mail.*

The author is grateful to his family and his many friends for
their help in bringing this project to fruition. Special thanks to
Sylvia Leigh for bringing the book alive and to Mabel Foye
for the front cover.

CONTENTS

CONFESSION
It pleasures me to tell a tale,

THE MISFIT   1
Said baby camel to his ma:

KEVIN'S LEGACY   3
Oul Kevin was in great demand

NED'S ASS   6
"You shouldn't strike the little ass,"

PADDY'S MEDICINE   7
Oul Paddy had been very ill,

THE NIT NURSE   10
The teacher in the village school,

ACH, AH'M ONLY MIDDLIN'   13
Sitting on the Derry bus,

THE MISSION PRIEST   17
The grey haired Mission Priest stood up

THE MAN WITH SILVER HAIR   23
I drove him to the cemetry,

MY HERITAGE   27
My dad's been dead since sixty-six,

THE PLUMBER   30
The doctor had been out to dine

CANINE CAPERS   31
Now Father Murphy lost his dog,

FLASHIN' FIDO   32
'Twas Saturday night in the little ole town;

THE LIMERICK   36
The limerick tends to make us smile

INHERITANCE   37
The little farm at Mulnaslin

THE BALLAD OF THE RIVER MOURNE   38
The Mourne begins not far below

THE BALLAD OF THE GLEBE ANGLING CLUB   43
Whilst fishing in the river Finn,

THE MAN FROM LEGFORDRUM   46
In Legfordrum I met a man,

MAD MATILDA   48
'Twas more than fifty years ago, when he was just a lad,

MY FATHER'S DOUGLAS BRIDGE   53
My father came from Douglas Bridge,

THE BRIDGE   56
The little river, cool and clear,

O'REILLY'S LETTER   59
"Please send a pair of Mongeese,"

ROMAN HOLIDAY   60
The first time ever Pat and Mick

THE OLD SCHOOL PHOTOGRAPH   62
(Liscreevaghan)
I found an old school photograph,

FARE YOU WELL
"It pleasures me to tell a tale,"

CONFESSION

It pleasures me to tell a tale,
* Or have one told to me,*
And so I've hit the lyric trail
* At fifty eight plus three;*
With lays no one would ever dare
Regard as fine poetic fare.

For I am just a common guy
* Who loves the lilt of rhyme;*
I've never penned a verse that I
* Could not persuade to chime.*
The brand of verse regarded 'free'
Never has appealed to me.

Fate gave me a rhyming pen,
* For which I am beholden,*
Although I grumble now and then
* And wish the nib was golden.*
This pen of mine would never spin
A yarn to equal 'Gunga Din'.

Yes, rhyming can be lots of fun,
* And bring much satisfaction;*
It's verses that I haven't done
* That drive me to distraction.*
But I'll keep rhyming and pretend
I'm satisfied with what I've penned.

THE MISFIT

Said baby camel to his ma:
  "Why have I got such feet?
They seem to be a handicap
  When walking in the street."

The mammy camel smiled and said:
  "You have to understand,
Your feet were made especially
  For walking in the sand.
In those enormous desert wastes,
  When others lose their grip,
You and I will travel on,
  We're called 'The Desert Ship'."

The baby camel tried again,
  This time a little soppy,
"Please mammy won't you tell me why
  My eyelids are so floppy?"

"When travelling in the desert
  You have to realise,
The winds can blow the sand about
  And irritate your eyes.
When other beasts and even men
  Are lagging far behind,
Those floppy lids will do their job,
  You won't be rendered blind."

That's very well," the baby said,
  "But I feel such a chump,
So mammy won't you please explain
  Why I have got a hump?"

"Now here again," his mammy said,
  "You have to bear in mind,
For storing precious water
  That's specially designed.
When others falter in the heat,
  And fail to stay alive,
We have a private reservoir
  So we will both survive."

Said baby camel to his ma:
  "I'm glad I'm just like you,
But won't you tell me, mammy dear,
  Why I'm in Dublin Zoo?"

KEVIN'S LEGACY

Oul Kevin was in great demand
  Because he had for long
Been recognised for counting sheep,
  And never being wrong.
You'd see him on a market day,
  Beside the biggest pen,
Concentrating very hard
  And nodding now and then.

And even on occasion,
  Though drovers did their best,
The sheep would break formation
  And scamper east and west;
But Kevin never faltered,
  His eye would never fail,
He'd get his calculation
  Bang upon the nail.

Because such feats of counting
　No one had ever seen,
They brought a maths professor
　Down from Stephen's Green;
But viewed from every angle
　His efforts were in vain,
This style of calculating
　He just could not explain.

But then, alas, oul Kevin
　Was taken very ill,
And sent for his solicitor
　To notarise his Will;
And then he called his only son,
　Whose name was Kevin too,
Said he: "Of all my worldly goods,
　I leave the best to you."

Now Kevin Junior listened up
　For, though his heart was sad,
He always had a hankering
　To emulate his dad.
He had to have the formula,
　His dad was fading fast,
And then oul Kevin spoke again
　Before he breathed his last.

"That special way of countin'
  When roundin' up the sheep,
Is just a very simple trick
  An' now it's yours to keep.
There's really nuthin' to it,
  You'll always get the score,
If you just simply count the legs
  An' then divide by four."

NED'S ASS

"You shouldn't strike the little ass,"
  Said Father Pat to Ned,
Who doffed his cap in reverence
  And also scratched his head.

"What ails ye Father don't you know
  Them asses can be lazy?
That's why you'll see me now and then
  Use the stick on Daisy."

"Don't give me that," said Father Pat,
  "You know 'twas one of them
That Our Redeemer, Jesus, rode
  Into Jerusalem."

"I'll take yer word for that," said Ned,
  "Because yerself has said it,
But if he'd had this ass of mine
  He never would have made it!"

PADDY'S MEDICINE

Oul Paddy had been very ill,
  He hadn't slept for days,
So Bridget called the doctor in
  To check on his disaise.

The doctor took his stethoscope
  And checked him fore an' aft.
Said Bridget: "Can you cure him, Sir,
  Before he drives me daft?"

Oul Paddy groaned impatiently:
  "Shure woman won't you cease;
Just let the doctor do his job
  An' lave us both in peace."

The doctor nodded knowingly,
  Then unto Paddy said:
"You've got a chest infection,
  You'll have to stay in bed."

"I guessed as much," said Bridget,
　That's more than just a cold;
Now listen to the doctor
　An' do as you are told.

"If it wasn't for me, doctor,
　He wouldn't be alive,
For when it comes to medicines
　He'll neither lead nor drive!"

Oul Paddy kept his temper,
　Albeit only just,
For interfarin' wimmin
　Annoyed him fit to bust.

"These tablets I'm prescribing,"
　Said Doctor Michael Hayes,
"Should cure the inflammation;
　Take two alternate days."

Now Bridget eyed him quizzically,
　And so indeed did Pat,
Said she: "This word 'alternate'
　Now what is meant by that?"

"It's easy," said the doctor,
　"Just think of it like this,
As two a day then skip a day;
　Be careful not to miss."

Both Pat and Bridget understood
  This alternate description,
Then Bridget hurried to the store
  With Doctor Mike's prescription.

The doctor was astounded
  When, two weeks to the day,
Bridget called to tell him
  That Pat had passed away.

"Now did he take the tablets?"
  He earnestly enquired.
"If he followed my instructions
  He shouldn't have expired."

"Now shure I told him doctor
  Them tablets were the best,
That two a day then skip a day
  Would soon clear up his chest."

The doctor said: "I cannot see
  Why he did not get better.
You followed my instructions
  Right to the very letter."

"Ah, that I did," said Bridget,
  "I took them home and drilled 'im.
Them tablets might have done the job -
  Shure 'twas the skippin' killed 'im!"

THE NIT NURSE

The teacher in the village school,
  Well qualified in art,
Had called the class together
  And was just about to start.
A lesson in the finer points
  Was what she had in mind,
But many of the boys and girls
  Were otherwise inclined.

Said little Bridie Donovan:
  "Please Miss it isn't fair,
Them naughty boys behind us
  Keeps tuggin' at our hair."
Then Mary Ann McCafferty,
  A buxom ten year old,
Plants a perfect bunch of knuckles
  On a lad who's overbold.

"They'll never stop their nonsense Miss,
  Until you use the cane,"
Said Theresa Moriarty
  Just before she howled in pain;
And little Paddy Docherty,
  Who's pinched her ample south,
Lookin' like a piece of butter
  Wouldn't melt inside his mouth.

"I won't stand any more of this,"
  Miss Madigan opines,
And flayed the air to try to scare
  That bunch of philistines.
"I'll send for Mr Cassidy;
  You'll have yourselves to blame."
But they paid her scant attention -
  And then the Nit Nurse came!

The pupils stared in disbelief
  And silence hit the room,
And faces that exuded fun
  Were now recording gloom.
The prospect of 'a letter home'
  Filled each with apprehension
As Nurse Malone surveyed the scene
  And added to the tension.

Those naughty boys had lost the urge
  To tug on pony tails,
And here and there a furtive glance
  At dirty finger nails;
And little Mickey Finnegan
  Could not resist a scratch,
The kind of thing that indicates
  A "lodger" in the thatch.

"Now boys and girls, this afternoon,
  I'd like to talk to you
About the need for cleanliness
  In everything you do.
For germs will live and multiply
  Wherever there is dirt,
So wash your hands and cut your nails,
  And often change your shirt.

"Come tell me now," said Nurse Malone,
  Addressing 'Curly' Brown,
A little gent from head to toe,
  In spite of 'hand-me-down'.
"How long you wear a shirt my boy,
  Stand up and tell the class" -
Which brought the ready-made reply:
  "An inch below me ass!"

ACH, AH'M ONLY MIDDLIN'

Sitting on the Derry bus, in the Omagh
bus depot,
I heard this conversation a lot of
years ago;
An' Ah thought Ah'd better tell you for Ah'm
sure you'd like to know.

"Ach, dammits, Jimmy, how're ye doin'?
Are ye in the town the day?"
"Ach, Ah'm only middlin', Mrs Breen,
This cowl won't go away.
Ah've had it now a month or more,
It's settled on me chest,
There's days Ah'm feelin' rightly
An' there's days Ah'm naw the best."

"Lord bliss me sowl now Jimmy,
There's a lot o' that about.
Hiv ye been tay see the doctor?
We don't want ye conkin' out."
"Shure Ah hiv no faith in doctors
An' Ah'll tell ye, Mrs Breen,
They always bury their mistakes,
That's why they're niver seen."

"Ach, dammits, Jimmy, Ah don't know,
They do the best they can;
Ah'm still wi' doctor so and so -
But he's a quare wee man."
"My doctor's killed wi' ulcers,
He canne cure 'imsel'.
Ah'll stick tay whiskey, Mrs Breen,
An' let them go tay hell."

"Isn't it terbil weather, Jimmy,
Lashin' night an' day?"
"Aw, terbil weather, Mrs Breen,
We'll al' be washed away."
"Aw, terbil weather, Jimmy,
There's no end tay the rain."
"Aw, terbil weather, Mrs Breen,
Luk, there it's on again!"

"Lord bliss me sowl now Jimmy,
Is it niver goin' tay stap?"
"There's not wan farmer, Mrs Breen,
Who'll hiv a daisent crap."
"Shure ivery place is boggin', Jimmy."
"Aye, boggin', Mrs Breen."
"It's terbil weather, Jimmy."
"Ach, the worst Ah've iver seen."

"Ah hope it settles, Jimmy,
Before it is too late."
"The cattle's starvin', Mrs Breen,
Jist plouterin'* roun' the gate."
"Lord bliss me sowl now Jimmy,
Is it niver goin' tay end?"
"We'll al' be drounded, Mrs Breen,
If the weather disne mend."

"Be God, yer right now Jimmy,
We'll be headin' fur the hills.
They say the very pirdies
Is rottin' in the drills."
"Aye, jist this mornin', Mrs Breen,
Ah wuz sayin' tay the wife,
Ah've niver seen such weather
In al' me livin' life."

* tramping

"How is she these days, Jimmy?"
"Ach, shure she's up an' down;
She harley iver laves the house,
Not even tay the town.
Now she's a good example
Where them doctors is tay blame,
Since she had that hypersectomy
She's niver been the same."

"Ach, give 'er my regards Jimmy."
"Ah will surely Mrs Breen.
She affen talks about the time
Yez both lived in Drumqueen."
"Aye, them wuz quare oul times, Jimmy,
When we were girls together.
We niver used to worry then
About sich things as weather."

"Shure Ah meant tay ask ye, Mrs Breen,
How is the boss 'imsel'?"
"He's as thran* as iver, Jimmy,
But he's keepin' very well.
Ye hiv tay watch yer P's and Q's,
Or else 'e'll rise a row -
Ah, we'll soon be movin', Jimmy,
Here's the driver comin' now."

* Awkward

THE MISSION PRIEST

The grey haired Mission Priest stood up
  And slowly made his way,
Up to the altar rails and there
  He knelt awhile to pray.
The silent congregation watched
  As he stood up once more,
And looked towards the pulpit steps,
  Then slowly crossed the floor.

"It isn't my intention friends
  To lecture or to preach;
No bible theme have I prepared,
  No homily or speech.
Instead, with your indulgence,
  I would like to tell a story,
And leave it there without comment
  On Godly Might and Glory.

"A heavy battle raged around
    A little town in France,
And many British soldiers knew
    They didn't stand a chance;
Outnumbered nearly three to one,
    And also short on tanks,
Five hundred fighting men were lost
    Forever to the ranks.

"A group of seven gallant men
    Volunteered to try
To penetrate the German lines,
    But four were doomed to die.
The three remaining volunteers
    Were helpless as they saw
The remnants of the Company
    Preparing to withdraw.

"For nearly seven hours they
    Were stranded on a ridge,
Until the cloak of darkness
    Brought them safely to the bridge.
They travelled fast into the night
    Until, at dawn, they came
To the Church of St Helena,
    From whom it got its name.

"Tired and dishevelled,
  But not to God inclined,
They went inside the little church
  Where each one spoke his mind.
One pointed to the Crucifix
  As scornfully he said:
'If You're supposed to love the world
  Why are my comrades dead?'

"Another tired soldier
  Knelt beside a pew,
And pressed his rifle to his cheek;
  His aim was swift and true.
'It's my belief religion is
  A lot of bluff and lies -
Behold! I've drilled a hole between
  The Great Redeemer's eyes!'

"The other soldier of the three
  Observed upon the shot,
Then slowly raised his rifle
  And picked himself a spot.
He squeezed the trigger gently
  And played the marksman part;
The instrument responded
  With a bullet through the heart.

"The lad who scorned the Crucifix,
　　Not to be outdone,
Leaned himself against the wall
　　And loaded up his gun.
Though bitter and resentful
　　His comrades forced a laugh,
When he almost missed the target
　　And shot a foot in half.

"He marched up to the Crucifix
　　And stood in mock salute:
'If you're so good at miracles
　　Repair your broken foot!
We don't believe in heaven
　　And we've had our share of hell,
So, if you've no objection,
　　We'll rest here for a spell!'

"The hour was approaching noon
　　As each picked up his pack,
And moved outside the little church
　　And then, a rifle crack!
The soldier who was first to shoot
　　Lay in the churchyard, dead,
With a sniper's bullet neatly
　　In the centre of his head!

"The two remaining volunteers
  Hurried back inside
And gazed upon the Crucifix -
  Their shock was hard to hide;
The bullet hole between the eyes,
  That each of them had seen,
Had disappeared without a trace
  As though it hadn't been!

"Undecided what to do
  Each at the other stared,
Then faintly in the distance
  A rumbling could be heard.
They climbed the spire steps and there,
  About a mile away,
The Company was coming back
  To fight another day.

"With reinforcements moving up
  The British troops held back,
Until the message came to say:
  'We're ready to attack!'
Then once more to the battlefield,
  Where many friends had died,
The two joined in with hundreds more
  Advancing side by side.

"The fight had scarcely started
  When the marksman from the church
Was seen by his companion
  To decline in wounded lurch.
'A perforated ventricle,'
  Was how they said he died,
The chap whose bullet pierced the heart
  Of Jesus Crucified!

"And so, before my story ends,
  Once more I say to you,
I leave it there without comment
  Although it's gospel true.
You'd like to know about the third?
  Good brethren, let us pray,
That soldier lad, whose aim was bad,
  Limped up here to-day!"

THE MAN WITH SILVER HAIR

I drove him to the cemetry,
  He thanked me for the ride,
Then as he walked towards the gate
  He faltered in his stride;
And held the little churchyard wall
  Before he went inside.

He walked along the winding path
  For twenty yards or so,
And, as I followed close behind,
  I watched him slowly go
From grave to grave expectantly,
  Within each hallowed row.

He halted by a faded stone,
  His head was bent and grey,
Two roses red were in his hand
  And then I heard him say:
"Oh Mary, won't you please forgive."
  And then he knelt to pray.

The evening sun was sinking
  As that man with silver hair,
Knelt, oblivious of the world,
  In fervent, silent prayer;
Then gently touched the mossy stone
  And placed the roses there.

I moved a dozen yards away,
  Not wishing to intrude,
And watched him as he cupped his hands,
  Then once again he stood,
And slowly trod the little path
  Towards a bench of wood.

We sat together for a while
  And then he said to me:
"Just fifty years ago today,
  When I was twenty-three,
I laid my darling Mary there
  With baby Rose Marie.

"We loved each other dearly
  And I recall with pride,
Within that little church up there
  When we stood side by side;
As my lovely childhood sweetheart
  Became my lovely bride.

"A happy lad and lass were we,
  I well recall the day,
Our happiness was multiplied
  When she came home to say:
'You're going to be a father, John,
  Our child is on the way.'

"The days and weeks went dancing by,
  Each hour was a joy,
We laughed a lot and talked of names
  For either girl or boy;
And vowed no power in the land
  Our true love could destroy.

"But when the fateful hour came
  The doctor shook his head:
'There is no way to save them both,'
  And then my Mary said:
'Our little baby has to live,
  Please let me die instead.'

"She gave her life to save our child,
  But it was not to be;
An hour after Mary died
  We christened Rose Marie
And laid her by her mother's side -
  I wished it could be me.

"I felt so empty and alone,
  Aye, sorry was my plight,
As I relived a thousand times
  The horror of that night;
Then an uncle in America
  Offered me respite.

"These fifty years that I've been gone,
  Since Mary passed away,
I've been involved in real estate
  In Boston, USA -
And now a lonely millionaire
  Is sitting here today."

We sat in silence for a while,
  He shook my hand and then
He walked along the winding path
  Towards the grave again;
And I felt that he was soon to go
  The way of mortal men.

There's a grave in County Leitrim,
  But please don't ask me where,
For Mary and her little girl
  Are sleeping peaceful there -
With another name upon the stone,
  The man with silver hair.

MY HERITAGE

My dad's been dead since sixty-six,
  I well recall the day
His tired body heaved a sigh
  Before he passed away.
Then ten years on the angels came
  When mum gave up the fight;
With heavy heart I still recall
  The phone call in the night.

Like many Irish parents
  They had laboured long and hard,
And battled with the elements,
  With often scant reward;
And, like many Irish parents,
  In importance next to God,
Was making sure the family
  Was always fed and shod.

Throughout the nineteen-forties
  We knew the golden rule
Was porridge in our bellies
  As we trundled off to school;
And often in the afternoon
  We'd short-cut through the bog,
To rendezvous with Irish stew
  Or poundies* or egg nog**.

*   Mashed potatoes, onion and butter
** A spicey omelette

And in the years from thirty-nine
  To nineteen-forty-five,
I well recall some families
  Whose men did not survive;
And how the dreaded telegram
  Would drive them to distraction -
Three fateful words upon a page
  Said simply "Killed in Action."

Through thick and thin and tragedies
  My mum and dad would cope,
And then the nineteen-fifties brought
  The great decade of hope.
But one by one we moved away
  And left them all alone,
Though now and then we would return
  With children of our own.

My mother loved us every one,
  We dearly loved her too,
And though he never said as much
  Our father's love we knew;
And many of our children
  Still recall with pride
Their many happy holidays
  At gran and grandad's side.

In Newtownstewart and Sion Mills,
  And all around Strabane,
I have a host of relatives -
  There's hundreds in the clan;
And every year I tell myself
  I'll journey o'er the foam,
And spend a happy holiday
  Amongst the folks back home.

I know they'll make me welcome
  And my heart will jump for joy,
To see the roads and byways
  Where I wandered as a boy.
But my most important visit
  Will be to Melmount where
My mum and dad are sleeping,
  And I'll kneel and say a prayer.

THE PLUMBER

The doctor had been out to dine
On T-bone steak and claret wine.
Returning home his wife was shocked
To find the toilet bowl was blocked.

But when the plumber had been phoned
He ranted first and then he moaned:
"The hour now is very late,
I'm sure that toilet bowl can wait."

"I must insist," the doctor said,
"Your business is consumer-led.
My plumbing friend, you must agree,
In that you're just the same as me."

Reluctant plumber, Tom O'Toole,
Agreed to play it by the rule.
"There may be truth in what you say
So I will now be on my way."

The plumber tapped the toilet bowl,
Then dropped two aspirin in the hole.
"Now if that doesn't ease the pain
By morning call me in again!"

CANINE CAPERS

Now Father Murphy lost his dog,
  Which caused him much distress,
And all day long around the town
  He searched without success.

He told the tale to everyone
  That he chanced to meet,
And then he saw McCafferty
  Digging up the street.

To see a grown man in tears
  For Pat was something novel,
And so he stopped and leaned himself
  Upon his navvy shovel.

"Now have you seen my little dog?"
  The tearful Father cries,
"He's snowy white with one black patch
  Over both his eyes."

"A black patch over both his eyes?
  Be japers, man," says Pat,
"I'm not surprised your dog is lost
  When handicapped like that."

FLASHIN' FIDO

'Twas Saturday night in the little ole town;
A handful of drifters was kinda hangin' aroun';
Some music was escapin' from The Star Saloon
From an ole pianer that was way out o' tune.

Then a hootin' an' a hollerin' an' shootin' in the air
Came Hank an' his boys from the Circle and Square.
They hitched their horses outside The Star,
Still a hootin' an' a hollerin' an' headed for the bar.

As ramrod Pete kicked a batwing door
An' ole hound dog crossed the bar room floor.
Pete pulled his gun with a loud guffaw
An' then he ventilated that hound dog's paw.

As bartender Pat was seein' to the boys
Along came the Sheriff investigatin' noise.
"Now listen up men you'd better calm down,
We don't like shootin' in this here town."

"Ah come on now Sheriff there's no harm done,
Me an' ma boys we wuz just havin' fun.
What Pete's been a doin' ain't against no law;
He just shot a hole in a hound dog's paw."

"Ah'm tellin' you guys an' Ah'm tellin' you plain,
You'd better not fire them guns again.
You've been workin' hard an' you've earned your ale,
But just keep thinkin' 'bout me an' ma jail."

Just four weeks later in that little ole town,
A handful of drifters was kinda hangin' aroun';
Some music was escapin' from The Star Saloon
From an' ole pianer that was way out o' tune.

Then a hootin' an' a hollerin' an' shootin' in the air
Came Hank an' his boys from the Circle and Square.
They hitched their horses outside The Star,
Still a hootin' an' a hollerin' an' headed for the bar.

As ramrod Pete kicked a batwing door,
There was no hound dog on the bar room floor.
Said foreman Hank with a loud guffaw:
"Where's that ole hound dog with the two-toed paw?"

Them cowpokes howled till they drowned the tune
From that ole pianer in The Star Saloon.
They howled some more when the barman said:
"He ain't been around - p'raps 'es dead."

The batwings parted an' then from the night,
A strange lookin' guy stepped into the light;
With guns on his hips an' specs on his nose -
'Twas that ole hound dog with the missin' toes!

The noise died down as Fido stood there,
Just eyein' them boys from the Circle and Square.
"This here's gotta be some kinda joke,"
Said foreman Hank - then the hound dog spoke:

"Ah'm an ole hound dog an' Ah limp when Ah walk -
Ah guess ye didn't know that dogs can talk.
Ah'm a totin' these guns an' Ah'm itchin' to draw,
Ah'm lookin' fur the guy who shot ma paw!"

THE LIMERICK

The limerick tends to make us smile
And has been with us quite a while;
  There's seldom been
  An evergreen
With such distinctive style.

And most folk will from time to time
Have dallied with this little rhyme;
  Both poet pure
  And bard obscure
Have welcomed its familiar chime.

They say that Harold Wilson too,
With lots of other things to do,
  Took up his pen
  At Number Ten
To write a five line verse or two.

And I've compiled at least a score
(It could be even twenty-four)
  Both bad and good
  And sometimes rude
And if I'm spared I'll write some more.

INHERITANCE

The little farm at Mulnaslin
  Is going to the dogs,
Ever since old Paddy Flynn
  Upped and popped his clogs.
The lazy son he left behind
To till the soil was not inclined.

Now Paddy was a daisent man,
  If ever there was one,
He worked that little piece of land
  Come hail, come rain, or sun.
For sixty years as man and boy
That holding was his pride and joy.

But now, alas, just four years on,
  Since Paddy passed away,
The tractor, cows and pigs have gone,
  The son is on the way.
A lifetime's honest toil he gave;
He must be turning in his grave.

Some say it is the alcohol,
  Some say the gambling game,
And others have no view at all
  Or won't apportion blame;
And others say it's just because
He's not the man his father was.

THE BALLAD OF THE RIVER MOURNE

The Mourne begins not far below
  The famous hill of Moyle,
Then travels north a dozen miles
  And then becomes the Foyle;
And in between the market towns
  Of Newtown and Strabane,
The nearest thing to Paradise
  For any fisherman.

How often in my younger days,
  Before I crossed the foam,
I played a silver salmon from
  The banks of Vaughan's Holm;
And often by The Hatchery
  I poached before I ran,
To hide from 'Covey' Morris,
  Along by Buneyban.

I've beached a few by McElreas
  And oftentimes I dream
About exciting escapdes,
  By good old Doaks's Stream;
Then on towards that lovely spot
  Where Derg and Mourne meet -
And the ghost of Henry Robinson
  Is silently on beat.

And then just half a mile away -
  It fills me with delight,
My father's favourite stomping ground,
  The Feddans, looms in sight;
With the ghosts of Captain Herdman,
  And John Buchanan too,
And poor old 'Monkey' Patton,
  To mention but a few.

How well do I remember,
  When fishing by the Linn,
My life was nearly ended
  When I tripped and tumbled in;
And how my elder brother
  Was on hand to pull me out,
Still clinging to my fishing rod
  And two-pound salmon trout.

By Nelson's Stream and Carney
  I've landed quite a few,
And mostly I was poaching -
  But that's between us two;
And then we move two hundred yards,
  Where cousin Tom and I,
Dodged old Pat the bailiff
  On the banks of Mulvin Bigh.

 Still dodging Pat McGuigan,
  And the anglers from Strabane,
We often used to plunder
  The Burnfoot and The Pan;
Then on to Basil Brooke's domain,
  We knew we often could
Land a fish and then retreat
  To hide in Liskey Wood.

Pool Archie, by Victoria Bridge,
  Is always worth a throw,
And Nestles is a pleasant spot
  Where many anglers go.
I've landed fish in both of these,
  By minnow, fly, and spoon -
I even caught a 'Springer'* once
  Three weeks this side of June.

Then moving on beyond The Bigh
  The river gathers steam,
To become the raging torrent
  That is known as Paddy's Stream.
There many a Sion fisherman
  Has passed the hours away,
And little Patsy Neeson
  Used to fish there every day.

The river settles down again
  And travels smooth and calm,
Beneath the span of Camus Bridge
  To constitute The Dam;
And then it travels slow and deep,
  By tree lined banks austere,
To where it flows then separates
  Between The Lade and Weir.

* A Spring Salmon

And then there is The Gravenue
  Where anglers have their fun,
But only on occasions when
  There's salmon on the run.
Then on towards The Blackstone
  The river flows and bends,
And makes its way towards Strabane
  To where its journey ends.

Dear friends, the memories I recall
  Span forty years or more -
A score and ten of these I've spent
  Upon a foreign shore.
But miles apart could never dim,
  And time could not erase,
My memories of the river where
  I spent such happy days.

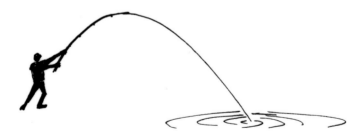

THE BALLAD OF
THE GLEBE ANGLING CLUB

Whilst fishing in the river Finn,
  In nineteen-fifty-nine,
Our thinking ran towards a plan
  We hoped would turn out fine.
Glebe fishermen were gathered when
  The next year had begun;
Give each his due with pledges true
  Foresworn by every one.

John Boyle was there as also were
  McCallions Tom and Hugh,
The Neeson brothers, Hugh and Pat,
  And brother Eddie too;
And beaming pride was Jim McBride,
  Likewise 'Eel' Cairns his pal;
Those were the 'Eight' - six now 'the late',
  The Good Lord rest them all.

By lampost light on a winter's night,
  Beside the Urney Road,
The plans were laid and dues were paid
  Within the angler's code.
We sowed the seeds, then signed the deeds
  On a cold and frosty morn;
To each his part in a humble start
  Glebe Angling Club was born.

For what it's worth a clod of earth
  Is what the Glebe word means;
Those men who trod that famous sod
  Now view celestial scenes.
Come soon or late a similar fate
  Awaits the two who tarry;
The Founding Men will meet again,
  But not beside 'The Karry.'

The Good and Great will tolerate
  In that Regime Divine,
Inherent need within the breed,
  The sons of rod and line.
On 'Opening Day' the Lord will say:
  "Your earthly whims I'll pardon;
I see each mind is still inclined
  To head for Killygordon."

'Eel' Cairns will stand by portals grand
  And beam through outer space,
A toothy grin towards the Finn,
  That other hallowed place;
Then round the gate the 'Founding Eight'
  Will congregate with pride;
The Neesons true, McCallions too,
  John Boyle and Jim McBride.

GLEBE ANGLING CLUB

******

25th ANNIVERSARY
1960 - 1985

*****

The Founding Members were:

Mr. THOMAS McCALLION
Mr. HUGH NEESON
Mr. PATRICK NEESON
Mr. HUGH McCALLION
Mr. EDWARD NEESON
Mr. JOHN BOYLE
Mr. EDWARD CAIRNS
Mr. JAMES McBRIDE

*****

Honorary Membership is conferred on all
Founding Members in appreciation for all
the enjoyable years of angling they
provided to all members
past and present.

For and on behalf of the Club:

Hon. Secretary

THE MAN FROM LEGFORDRUM

In Legfordrum I met a man,
Who offered me his boney hand,
   'Twas early in the morning.
I still can see his features yet
As he held out a scrawny mitt,
   Then vanished without warning!

His haunted eyes were set within
A sallow face with pointed chin,
   His body sagged and bent.
His origin I know not where,
I only know that he was there,
   I know not where he went!

Some three decades had passed and then
I saw that self-same man again,
   Beside my own front door;
But once again to my surprise,
And right before my very eyes,
   There he was no more!

That wizened wretch from Legfordrum
Had travelled all the way to Brum;
   I only wish I knew,
Why twice in thirty years that he
Should manifest himself to me,
   And what was I to do?

THE MAN FROM LEGFORDRUM
(THE SEQUEL)

Another seven years had gone and then that man had come,
Just as he promised in the note, the man from Legfordrum.
He sat across from where I sat, his ancient frame inclined,
"Come tell me sir," I bravely said, "Just what is on your mind?"

Then as the seconds ticked away he shifted in his chair,
Within my little study room and fixed me with a stare.
He pursed his lips and when he spoke to offer first his name,
The voice that echoed round the room belied his broken frame.

"Ah, she was such a bonnie lass but, as the years went on,
Her wedded chances slipped away, her mother too had gone.
We lived a lonely barren life, with very few to call,
My daughter Mary Jane and me back home in Donegal.

"Until that day in ninety-eight a would-be suitor came
Into our white-washed cottage and offered her his name.
A deal was struck and though it may seem very strange to some,
My daughter Mary Jane and me lit out for Legfordrum.

"We worked together as a team, the two of them and me,
Until rheumatic fever struck and I had ceased to be.
It was the busy harvest time and so they laid me down
At dead of night in Legfordrum in plain, unhallowed ground.

"The neighbours back in Donegal, who'd heard my time had come,
Assumed that I'd been laid to rest somewhere near Legfordrum.
And folk up there had been informed I rested 'neath the loam
Of my own native county amongst the folks back home.

"A silver birch tree marks the spot and, though it's grand and tall,
Beneath its shade there languishes oul Matt from Donegal."
He handed me a tattered map saying, "If you'd be so kind,
One hundred golden sovereigns upon my corpse you'll find."

I scrutinised that crumpled map but I remembered not
The countryside surrounding the indicated spot.
The bridge above the little burn, not far from such a brae,
Was somewhere I would visit soon, at least to kneel and pray.

We sat in silence for a while before he spoke again,
Ere he dissolved into the night he made his feelings plain.
"Upon my friends, of whom you're one, I will not cease to call
Until my bones are re-interred back home in Donegal."

Hugh McCallion

See page 46

And now another ten years on
That man, again, has been and gone,
　　And still I know not where.
That bag of bones had travelled far -
Tonight the mirror in my car
　　Revealed him sitting there!

Those haunted eyes that dwelt within
A sallow face with pointed chin,
　　Were right behind my seat.
"Who are you, friend?" I bravely said,
He answered not but wrote instead,
　　"I will explain when next we meet!"

I have it here in squiggled hand
And soon, perhaps, I'll understand
　　The message that he wrote.
I know not why, I know not when,
I only know we'll meet again,
　　Meanwhile, I'll keep the note!

MAD MATILDA

'Twas more than forty years ago, when he was
     just a lad,
He heard the tragic story of a woman
     labelled 'mad'.
The horror of the story filled the little
     lad with fear
And the person who related it was soon to
     disappear.

Most every house in that townland could
     boast a raconteur,
But every one regardin' 'her' was stricken
     dumb for sure;
And even though a number knew the
     circumstances well
The detail of the story they were not
     prepared to tell.

It seemed the wretched woman had played a
     normal part
Until her evil father started dabbling in
     'The Art';
And the ending of the story would suggest
     that this was so,
But the grim and gory details you'd be safer
     not to know.

Then as the years went drifting by the growing
    lad would find
That poor, demented, woman would return to
    haunt his mind;
And in the intervening years, from nine to
    seventeen,
From time to time reluctantly he'd visualise
    the scene.

From little lad to seventeen a man had
    almost grown
When he saw a competition advertised in
    'Ireland's Own'.
The request was for a story of the kind
    inducing fright,
So he took a book and pencil and went upstairs
    to write.

The story that had haunted him he started
    to relate,
And called it 'Mad Matilda' - his pencil
    couldn't wait.
He had, within an hour, penned a thousand
    words or more -
And then a ghostly presence opened up the
    bedroom door!

A chill ran up and down his spine: "Is someone
     there?" he said,
And then he saw the imprint of 'someone' on
     the bed.
He moved a little closer, then his courage
     quickly sank,
When he looked where he'd been writing and
     every page was blank.

The lad had got the message and he didn't
     try again,
Then nearly four years later aboard a Dublin
     train;
He found 'Matilda' published in an English
     magazine,
Exactly as he'd written it when he was
     seventeen.

Though he was sorely tempted to throw the
     thing away
He kept that periodical and read it
     every day;
And then he wrote a letter which brought
     this prompt reply,
"There's no story 'Mad Matilda' in our
     issue for July."

He read the letter over then checked
    the magazine
And sure enough Matilda was where she'd
    always been.
He read the opening paragraph then, much
    to his surprise,
The story started fading before his
    very eyes.

Perplexed and agitated he hurled it to
    the floor
And then he saw a photograph that wasn't
    there before.
He knelt beside the magazine, though feeling
    far from brave,
And saw a wild-eyed woman beside an
    open grave.

He grabbed that publication and, such was
    his desire,
He tore it into pieces and threw it on
    the fire;
Then watched with apprehension, and not a
    little fright,
As one by one the pieces disappeared
    from sight.

For twenty years, religiously, he left the
        tale alone,
Though now and then Matilda would make her
            presence known;
As either by illusion or subjugated fear,
That title would materialise and then
            would disappear.

He kept his scary secret then one
            fateful day
He felt a strange compulsion to write it
            come what may;
But for some unknown reason, which he
            couldn't understand,
The pen refused to function within his
            writing hand.

And though another twenty years have been
            and gone since then,
And nigh a hundred ballads have fallen
            from his pen,
He still has not succeeded, though many
            times he's tried,
To write about Matilda and how she lived
            and died.

Each time he tries to write it things go
    from bad to worse,
So he's finally decided he will try to
    break the curse.
**So Matilda please release me and I promise
    I will cease,**
**And let your troubled spirit have a chance
    to REST IN PEACE!**

MY FATHER'S DOUGLAS BRIDGE

My father came from Douglas Bridge,
  I keep in memory still,
The many tales he told to me
  About the old scutch mill;
And many another story too
  Of happy times he had,
Ticklin' trout in Douglas Burn
  When he was just a lad.

He spoke with some affection too,
  Although the work was hard,
Of cutting turf for Tommy Dick
  And scutching for Dan Ward;
And how, when he was twelve years old,
  He worked in Sion Mill,
Three days a week - the other two
  At school in Three Mile Hill.

He talked about the 'Student' Hood
  And other folk he knew,
Like Birse the tramp and 'Tie-the-Boy'
  And Charlie Francey too;
And blacksmith Jimmy Doherty,
  Who never thought it odd,
To disappear when 'on the tare'*
  And leave a horse half shod.

"God rest oul Biddy Faulkner,"
  My dad would often say -
She kept a little sweet shop
  At the foot of Knockroe brae;
And Coyles and Beatties taverns
  Were often called to mind,
To which the men of Douglas Bridge
  Were very well inclined.

'Tis but a glimpse I've given you
  Of Douglas long ago,
A part of life's rich tapestry
  My father used to know.
He passed away in sixty-six,
  I wonder what he'd say,
If heaven sent him back again
  To Douglas for a day.

* On the booze

THE BRIDGE

The little river, cool and clear,
  Meandered slowly down
To where it splashed across the weir,
  Before it passed the town;
And then it disappeared awhile
  Behind a little ridge,
Then flowed another quarter mile
  Before it reached the bridge.

The Council had prepared a plan,
  They hoped would be approved,
To build a modern river span
  And have the old removed.
But then a Conservation bloke
  Arranged a big petition,
Signed by near two hundred folk
  Opposed to demolition.

"A public meeting is the way,"
  The local paper stated,
"For everyone to have their say
  And have the thing debated.
The public have a right to know
  And to participation."
The Council were agreed and so
  Were those from Conservation.

A man from Dublin town was sent,
  A Civil Servant fella,
To organise the great event -
  With briefcase and umbrella.
The venue was the market hall,
  On Friday night at eight;
The Mayor would welcome one and all
  And start the great debate.

The meeting place was like a mart,
  They came from near and far,
By bicycle and ass and cart
  And some by motor car.
Some words of welcome from the Mayor,
  Who took his rightful place,
To run the meeting from the Chair
  And ventilate the case.

The Council man was first to speak,
  And well did he orate;
He could have rattled for a week
  But stopped at half-past-eight.
The other guy then took the floor,
  The one from Conservation,
And gave, just like the one before,
  An eloquent oration.

Then Mayor Delaney rose again,
  From where he had been sittin',
And pointed to where Paddy Kane
  Was chewin' plug and spittin'.
"Perhaps you'd like a word," said he,
  "I've been observing you
And, as you seem to disagree,
  Let's have your point of view."

Said Pat: "You have a flamin' scheme,
  Just go ahead an' toss it;
Such fuss about a blasted stream
  Shure I could piss across it!"
"You're out of order," ruled the Mayor,
  Said Pat: "'Tis right you are,
On second thought I do declare
  I could piss twice as far!"

O'REILLY'S LETTER

"Please send a pair of Mongeese,"
  Was what O'Reilly wrote,
Then realised his error
  And quickly tore the note.

He'd often chided others for
  Grammatical misuses,
And so he wrote another note,
  "Please send me two Mongooses."

This effort sounded even worse,
  He pondered but in vain,
The plural of the Mongoose
  Escaped his tired brain.

Perplexed by unavailing thought,
  Said he: "Aw what the hell!
Please send me one Mongoose," he wrote,
  "And send a mate as well."

ROMAN HOLIDAY

The first time ever Pat and Mick
Had been away from home
Was on a summer holiday;
A package trip to Rome.

The flight was most enjoyable,
The hostesses divine,
Not to mention fancy food
Washed down with lots of wine.

And when the plane had landed
They heard the Captain say:
"I hope you had a pleasant trip,
Enjoy your holiday."

The Courier was a Latin lass
Who spoke the English well,
And organised the transport to
The holiday hotel.

"Tomorrow is a busy day,"
The Latin lady said,
"I'll meet you at the Vatican
So don't be late in bed.

"The Vatican at 9 o'clock."
Said Pat: "Now right you are."
Said Mick: "You'd better ask her Pat,
The Smoke Room or the Bar?"

THE OLD SCHOOL PHOTOGRAPH
(Liscreevaghan)

I found an old school photograph,
　From fifty years ago,
And donned my spectacles to see
　How many I would know.
Imagine what a thrill it was
　For me to realise,
That thirty out of forty-one
　I still could recognise.

There was Pearl and Annie Russell,
　And brothers John and Bill,
Who travelled down from Clady Hood,
　Which we called 'Clady Hill'.
There was Dave and Freddie Canning,
　With Aidan Farrell as well,
And also Pat McMonigle
　And Sid and Albert Bell.

There was Angela McClintock,
　And also sister Dot,
As well as sister Rhona,
　Whose name I near forgot.
There was Bridie, Nell and William,
　From the family of McBride,
And pretty Maureen Kelly
　And brother Frank beside.

Then all the way from Douglas Bridge
  Came Frank and Noel Devine,
With older sister Kathleen
  Who was a friend of mine.
Then Johnnie Tracey, I recall,
  Who came from Douglas too,
And also Ed McSorley,
  Which leaves us just a few.

The Andersons were also there,
  Helen, Bertie and Kathleen,
And Mary Ellen Campbell
  Who journeyed from Killeen.
Then Kath and Charlie Doherty
  Makes the total twenty nine.
You say there is another one?
  The missing name is mine.

FARE YOU WELL

"It pleasures me to tell a tale,"
Was how this book began,
And though I'm well equipped to fail
I've done the best I can.
For rhyming is a dandy trade -
Albeit one that's poorly paid.

But that's not how we judge success,
And I have no pretence,
A better guide is happiness
Not merely pounds and pence.
So if my verses you've enjoyed
Then I've been gainfully employed.

My dear old mother used to say:
"You'll only waste your breath,
Unless you make them laugh or cry
Or scare them half to death."
For you, dear friend, if such it be,
I hope this book has done all three.

Now as we go our separate ways
I bid you fortune's cheer,
And hope you spare a little praise
For this poor balladeer;
And may this most sincere refrain
Endure until we meet again.